I0684796

Flesh *of My* *Thoughts*

Harry Best

Flesh of My Thoughts

Harry Best

Published by:
Harry Best
P.O. Box 21783
El Sobrante, CA 94820

Printed in the United States of America
Editing and design by Laurie Masters of Precision Revision

Best, Harry
    Flesh of my thoughts / by Harry Best;
        ISBN-13: 9780692934708
        ISBN-10: 0692934707

Words
Flesh of my thoughts
Food of my actions

Table of Contents

I. POETRY

II. LYRICS

III. SHORT STORIES

I
POETRY

Another Dance With You
(To Merrill on her death bed)

I'm waiting for another dance with you
That's what I'm visualizing
Can you see that day?
Real soon
Sliding feet
Swinging hips
Cheeks warm like mangoes in the sun
Swinging, swaying, sweating
To the rhythm of the drum
Don't stop that music
Don't stop that music
I'm waiting for another dance with you.

Awaken, Oh Father!

Awaken, oh Father!
Your dreams torment me
I am cast about by wind and storm.
You dream of lack
And I bear witness to the fact
You dream of doubt and fear
And I am tortured here
I knock at the rock of Golgotha
Sealed tight in your coffer
You sleep in this terror
Of stale thoughts in error
Waging destruction
And dispossession from your
Sweet resurrection.
Awaken, oh Father!

Now

My mind
A bank of pain
An account
Opened at the inauguration of reason
Accumulated interest of morality
To be spent only
Towards that blind inevitable investment
Death

Home Again

In our young years
We went home frequently,
Thinking we could barter
The chagrin of wistful days in exile
For happy times suspended in memory.
And we almost did.
Sweet seasonal fruit
A joyful jig
And moist flesh
Savored best without commitment.
Until sweet sorrow
Too soon relived
Stamped in a passport
Marked the end of the foray.

The Hierarchy

Where are you in the hierarchy?

At the feet?
Oppressed, repressed, depressed
Burning with desire to attain the crown?

Or at the head?
Engrossed, possessed, impressed
Paralyzed with fear that you might fall down

Or lost in the middle?
Tugged by the waves of polarity
Not knowing which way to go
Or what direction is the natural flow

What does it matter?
Where you are in the hierarchy?
But that you know your part
And play it to the end?

Vindication

Today I uncovered my soul
And there you were
Relieved that I had resigned to my vocation
Saying "I told you so."
But you had only stoked the embers of a faded guilt
I had lost memory of that stroke of genius
Suppressed from believing I was incomplete
     and only halfway there
Since then I have duplicated the feat numerous times
     with laurels
It was music that taught me to create new melodies
     to old progressions
And what I was privately ashamed of turned out to be
     the rule in school
Yes, sweet lyrical melodies are all that's expected of me
There are no new progressions
And those that exist are in the public domain
So sing words, sing
I'll never try another thing.

Why We Sing the Blues

Someone said that It,
Had a case of the blues
And wishing to validate It,
Extended to regions so far from It,
That It appeared to be It's opposite (Self).
At the end of the day,
It as Self,
Looked back on ItSelf in validation saying
"It is good."
That was the birth of duality,
Love and Hate.
And mankind was appointed as the medium for their resolutions.
Mankind being but a phase of ItSelf,
Extended into Self to validate It.
But confused by the reflection of It in Self,
And believing Self was primary,
Validated It's opposite.
A misdirected Love
Causing ill feelings of Hate
When validation is not forthcoming.
And so, we sing the blues.

The Belly of the Wave

In our youth
We challenged the sea
With its waves of unpredictability
Some we rode blissfully
And landed softly on the sandy shore
But a wily change in rhythm
Or a moment of misjudging
Left one caught in indecision
To flee or to surrender
To the mercy of the tumbler.
In time we learned the answer
Shared by a broken brother
Who knew that you'd be safe
Diving into the belly of the wave.

Resignation

I am prescribed to myself
My joys, my likes, my victories
My doubts, my fears, my failures
And though I seek at every turn
To right a wretched wheel
The journey leads but one way
To climb this cursed hill
One key assigned to manage
A promise keeps me bound
But for the hope of glory
I might have turned around.

Hierarchies

Step back from the trees
Now see the forest
A fabric of interwoven hierarchies
Plants, animals and man
In micro-conflicts of polar extremes
One motivated by fear
The other by desire
And as they trade places
"Truth" becomes a lie
And lies become the "truth"
Thus swings the pendulum
Ad infinitum

First Born Sacrifice

An infant turtle
Lay dead in the sand
Sinfully short of the flirting waves
That wet the lips of the shore.
Tracks of gratitude
Laid by scared siblings' fins
Mark a patterned trail
To the welcoming refuge of the sea.
But there she lay
A lifeless sun-scorched shell
A mini monument
To the sacrifice of the first born
Whose fate it is
To blaze a path with courage
Long on heart
But short on stamina.

To Holly Elder

Farewell pan soldier
I know we'll meet again
Someday
And I will know you
By the way
You hold your sticks
By your signature licks
And I'll embrace you
Once again
And we'll be jammin'
As we did in our last meeting

Return

I am descending from the sun
With the witch
Her broom, the bird of reason.
I come
That I might cast away this haunt
A nostalgic torment that compels me here.

I see smoke-painted hills
Rising from dark vaginal valleys
With rivers ejaculated
To the ocean's batik

The uncertainty of my expectations
Chides my erratic departure.
Past pains for future pleasure is my hope

Frozen in my childhood past
My memories thaw here
Where beaches smile
With lips of green starry palms
Their roots like cabled toes
Gripping tightly in the sand
Where the waves sneeze.

I arrive

Concoction

With a silver spoon
Take three drops from a bleeding moon
And chill
With the breath of night
Add the sweat of forty stars
Wiped from their brows
With the first sheet of dawn
Then to the west
To find
In the chalice of the ocean
Tears from a dying day
Churn
With a cricket's whistle
Or an earthworm's wriggle
Spread well
Onto the bread of life
Now taste.

Goddess of Earth's love

As I withdraw
From slurping water
Trickling down the crevices
Of your hillsides

As I recall how
Like waves we humped and thumped
On the submissive sands of passion

As I long again
To smell your warm fertility
In the sweet scent of spring flowers
And sing songs of seduction
In the whispered whistle of a swallow

I find the earth
Alive again
In your love.

Sunlife

The old man stood
At the edge of the waters of uncertainty
And stared into the golden sun
As it sunk slowly
Toward the horizon of his life.
Chagrin eclipsed his senses
And commanding that the sun stand still
He dove into a reflection
Of silver sunrises
And blazing afternoons
Of a more youthful, carefree time
That had entertained no vision
Of the imminent sunset.

II
LYRICS

Living in Your Dream

I

A player on the stage of life
My part is filled with
    toil and strife
Content to play it all the same
Since I was chosen for the game

And though sometimes
    I lose the tense
It's not because of
    false pretense
Don't look upon me
    with disdain
If I should call your
    name in vain

Refrain

I'm living in your dream,
    Yahweh
I'm living in your dream,
    Vau-Heh
Come and justify my soul

I'm living in your dream,
    Jah Jah
I'm living in your dream,
    Father
Come and glorify my soul

II

You crowned me Prince in
    death's domain
And promised when you
    come again

I'd shed this costly
    cross of wood

And join the saintly
    brotherhood

My weary soul 6,000 years
Of living through this
    veil of tears
But in the end I do esteem
I AM the dreamer
    and the dream

Refrain

I'm living in your dream,
    Yahweh
I'm living in your dream,
    Vau-Heh
Come and sanctify my soul

I'm living in your dream,
    Jah Jah
I'm living in your dream,
    Father
Come and glorify my soul

Refrain

I'm living in your dream,
    Yahweh
I'm living in your dream,
    Vau-Heh
Come and justify my soul

I'm living in your dream,
    Jah Jah
I'm living in your dream,
    Father
Come and glorify my soul

Pan Wisdom

Life is love
When you live
Just to give of yourself
Precious love
Like a blessing from above
Everything that you know
You are willing to show
    and more

Then there comes a time
When you reach to find
Extra love in your heart
You know you didn't
    have to care
But you did
And now you are
    who you are today

So with emotion strong
We celebrate this song
A soulful expression
And devotion
A humble oration
Of appreciation
Because today
We are thankful
    for this wisdom

Pan is love
Pan is life
Giving light from the heart
Endless bliss
Sticks and steel sing
    when they kiss
Giving inspiration
To this composition
Wisdom
Now I think of you
As I search to find
All the love in my heart
I want you to know
    how much I care
Darling dear
I will always be sincere

So with emotion strong
I dedicate this song
A joyful expression
Of pan passion
A humble oration
Of appreciation
Because today
(Like yesterday
And every day)
I am grateful
    for your wisdom

Where I Live

You can find me on happy
    mountain
Healthy like a bubbling
    fountain
Way above the mind-trick
    constrain
That's where I live

You can take imagination
Hitch it to a higher vision
And declare your destination
To where I live

When the valley is flooded
    down below
And it seems' like there's no
    place to go
Just go' within and say no more
Soon' you'll be knocking
    at my door

Let's keep it in our
    conversation
Feel it's more than just
    a notion
Gonna have a celebration
Here where I live

Come on up to happy mountain
Get giggly like a bubbling
    fountain
We'll look down on the
    mind-trick constrain
From where I live

Deep Purple

I

For many years
I've wondered why
These tears I cry

Wearing a smile
But all the while
The child chokes up inside

Tried to paint a picture
Of the words I want to say
Comes delusion and confusion
Then the vision of my mission
Fades away

II

When all the world was
    cast in red
I tried instead, (Deep Purple)
In search of fame
    I played the game
It all turned out the same

And in my darkest hour
As I turned to walk away
Caught a glimmer
    of the shimmer
Turned the corner,
    saw the colour
Of the day

III

And now at last
    my time has come
Can't run 'way from
    (Deep Purple)
I'll set the stage and take a page
From lessons of the sage

Knowing that a Sunday
Is only Monday's yesterday
I will praise Jah with the power
Till the colour of the hour
Is no more (Deep Purple)

Changed My Name

I

I used to hang my head and cry
Wondering when I would
    get by
But it'll be alright
Now I changed my name

I used to think I'd never win
Showing up short is such a sin
But it'll be alright
Now I changed my name

Setting my aim
Staking my claim
Fortune and fame
Falling short is a shame
But it'll be alright
Now I changed my name

Excuses are lame
Ain't no one to blame
Can't stay the same
Steppin' up on my game
It'll be alright
Now I changed my name

II

I used to worry night and day
Wishing that I would
    find a way
That would be alright
Since I changed my name

I used to think I'd never find
True happiness and
    peace of mind
But it'll be alright
Now I changed my name

Out with the old
In with the new
It's the only thing to do
When it'll be alright
If you change your name

I'm talking to you
Am I getting through
Tell me what you gonna do
Say it'll be alright
If you change your name

Wake Me Up

I

When will I awaken
When will I be born
Seems like I'm forsaken
Here in Albion

When will I see David
Know when he appears
Soon I will be severed
Cleft between the ears

So shake me up
Wake me up
Bring back the memory
    of what I used to be
Shake me up
Wake me up
Graced in your glory is
    where I long to be

II

Lived this life in famine
Hungry for your word
Wrestled night 'til morning
'til at last you heard

Excited by your promise
Faith won't let me fail
Love will be my premise
'til you lift up the veil

So shake me up
Wake me up
Bring back the memory of
    what I used to be
Shake me up
Wake me up
Graced in your glory is
    where I long to be

III

When will I awaken
When will I be born
I was ill-begotten
Here in Albion
When will I see David
They tell me he's my son
In a vision lucid
He and I are one

So shake me up
Wake me up
Bring back the memory
    of what I used to be
Shake me up
Wake me up
Graced in your glory is
    where I long to be

Love Sublime

I

Sitting in the station
Waiting for the train
To come and take me
    home again
Sweet anticipation
Sweeping through my brain
I feel impatient but
    I can't complain

Over at the counter
Checking one more time
If I'm on schedule for
    the northern clime
Heard the whistle blowing
Got to get in line
Cause we'll be boarding
One at a time

Next stop is Love Sublime
Get your things together
It's the end of the line
Be back in Love Sublime
Show them all you've got
And let your love light
    shine

II

Said the train's conductor
You been here before

Moving closer you'll
    remember more
It's been such a long time
Plumb gone out your mind
Day you left to learn about
    the southern clime

Like the man Nathaniel
I behold no guile
Checked his watch and then
    he flashed a smile
There'll be folks awaiting
Just to hear you tell
All the frightful things you
    learned in hell

Next stop is Love Sublime
You won't need to transfer
It's the end of the clime
We back in Love Sublime
Stay seated 'till you hit
The end of the line.

Dead stop it's Love Sublime
Got you back to where
    it all began
You're here in Love Sublime
Now behold the glory
Of the Master Plan.

Imagination

I

Life is like a melody
Dressed in nature's harmony
With the bass
    and the drummer
It's all held together
With pure Imagination

If your life should go off track
And it's a struggle
    coming back
Very soon you'll recover
If you use but one measure
Of pure Imagination

Bridge

I try so many ways
Working all my fingers
    to the bone
I cried so many days
Looking for the answer
Searching for the stone

II

If you really want to know
How to set your life aglow

In a deep meditation
Find the rock of creation
In your Imagination
So shine your light and
    let it show
Let your loving feelings flow
Singing praises to Jah Jah
And Mother Africa
In your Imagination

Bridge

Why try so many ways
Working all my fingers
    to the bone
Why cry so many days
Looking for the answer
Searching for the stone

III

If you really want to know
How to set your life aglow
In a deep meditation
Find the rock of salvation
In pure Imagination

Mary Had a Baby

I

Wild wind blows nobody
    knows
Whence it comes or
    where it goes
Woke to find that I'd been dead
And I was buried in my head

II

I rolled the stone and
    eased on out
Then I began to look about
I saw myself in deep distress
My body turning east to west

Why, Mary had a baby
    can't you see
Look how he's smiling
    back at me
I said to him
    "how is my lovely one?"
He called me Father,
    he's my son

III

Wise men came from
    o'er the fence
Bringing gifts of frankincense

They saw the star shine
    in the east
How could it be,
    Whose child is this?
I told them, Mary had a baby
    can't you see
Look how he's smiling
    back at me
I said to him
    "how is my lovely one?'"
He called me Father,
    he's my son

IV

Onto us a son is given
Onto us a child is born
What you gonna call him?
Wonderful!
What you gonna call him?
Counselor!
What you gonna call him?
Almighty Jah!
What you gonna call him?
Prince of Peace!
Prince of Peace!
Prince of Peace!

Thy Will Be Done

I place my faith
    upon the rock
Keeping it there
    around the clock
No doubt, no fear
Soon I'll be there
Victory is mine,
    I'm feeling fine

I keep my eyes
    upon the prize
There from the moment
    I arise
A mustard seed
Is all I need
For crumbling mountains
    to the sea

Listen to the lyrics in
    my little song
Put them into action and
    you can't go wrong

Get into the feeling of
    the wish fulfilled
For real,
Thy will be done

Children don't get weary
    'til your work is done
Keep the fire burning'
    'til you see the sun
Know that it will come
    and never doubt it will
Be still,
Thy will be done

Seedtime and harvest
    shall not cease
And what you sew
    you've got to reap
First came the promise
Then came the Law
I AM that I AM
    and nothing more

Break the Bread

I

Been with me right from
    the start
Not a minute from my heart
Searching blindly everywhere
Wish I'd known that
    you were there

II

Suffered seasons lost in time
Hoping with no aim defined
All too soon things fall apart
Should have known to
    trust my heart

Chorus

Break the bread and
    drink the wine
Makes my soul feel so refined
Things you said stuck
    in my mind
Now I know I am divine
Break the bread and
    drink the wine
Let my soul feel so refined
Left those worried thoughts
    behind
Now my life is so divine

III

Looking back it's plain to see
You were always there for me
Forgive me if I wasn't told
All that glitters is not gold
Thinking when you said to me
This whole world is vanity
Turned it upside down to see
Now the truth has set me free

Chorus

Break the bread and
    drink the wine
Makes my soul feel so refined
Things you said stuck in
    my mind
Now I know I am divine
Break the bread and
    drink the wine
Let my soul feel so refined
Since I looked within to find
In my life was love divine

The Drifter/My Happy Nest

I

A drifter came to town
Threw his weight around
Trying to upset my happy nest
I tried to pay no mind
Hoping he would find
It's useless to molest
My happy nest

II

The more the people said
The praise went to his head
He vowed then to possess
My happy nest
He rumbled through the town
Turned it upside down
And called from my rest
In my happy nest

Now, I'm peaceful,
    passive and permissive
Never raised a hand to
    hurt no one

But when I am turned to
    defenses
Reflexes prove the better
    of a man

III

I met him in the street
The crowd jumped to its feet
A showdown to contest
My happy nest
One shot between the eyes
The drifter fell and died
No more to infest
My happy nest

Though I'm peaceful
    passive and permissive
I'll never be a slave to anyone
And when I am on the
    defensive
Reflexes prove he better
    of a man.

III
SHORT
STORIES

The Mango Alawoz Tree
('Sa ou pa konet gran passe'w)

Playing "Police and Thieves"
De big boys like Ali, Zwav, and Hobbot would always be "thieves."
Tiwats like me, Gokaks, Polia, Wata and Peggi would be "police."
Thieves would go and hide,
And Tiwats went in search of them.
But, as usual, we would never find the thieves.
Dem fellas know places we don't know and we afraid to go.

But I had an idea.
If I could climb way up in de Mango Alawoz tree,
I could see de whole neighborhood,
All around; from Vigie to Martinique,
From de cemetery to Bob Harris and Ma Gooding's land.
Over to Skeete Hill, then by de field and Wally Downes home.
Vide Boutielle up to Boot Hill, all around.

So I climbed up de Mango Alawoz tree,
High up where I could see all around.
I looked, and looked, and looked, everywhere.
They were nowhere to be seen.

So I gave up
And making my way down de Mango Alawoz tree
I heard the giggling: "Hee hee hee hee hee …"

I raised my head and looked up.
Way up in the tallest part of the Mango Alawoz tree
The thieves were gathered in amusement.

Ritual Drama — Homecoming

RasAri: (Knock, knock, knock!)

Gatekeeper: Someone is knocking.
Master: Go ascertain who it is and why he knocks.
Gatekeeper: It will be done.

RasAri: (Knock, knock, knock!)

Gatekeeper: Who knocks? Identify yourself.
RasAri: It is I, RasAri, a long lost soul. I seek admittance.
Gatekeeper: Tarry, I will inform the Master.

Gatekeeper (to Master): A wanderer has found his way to the gates and requests admittance.
Master: Go determine whether he is qualified. And if he is, admit him. If he is not, direct him back to the crossroads.
Gatekeeper: It will be done.

Gatekeeper: The Master wants to know what led you to this door.
RasAri: For time immemorial I have searched for this place, and the path has led to this door.
Gatekeeper: Perhaps you are mistaken. The crossroads lead to many doors.
RasAri: There is no place else to go.
Gatekeeper: What makes you think you are qualified to enter here?

RasAri: I do not recall how I arrived at the dark crossroads. But in my struggles I was guided by a subtle light through many undulating passages, until it extinguished at your door. My journey is ended.

Gatekeeper: Then enter, my long lost brother.

RasAri: Forgive me if I have intruded on your celebrations. I will make myself obscure.

Master: Welcome RasAri, my long lost son. The celebration is in your honor. We have been expecting you. Everyone here has worked hard to win your passage.

ALL: **Let us rejoice!**

The Crib
For Chel

One of my earliest memories was of being in my crib having just awoken from sleep. I couldn't have been much more than twelve months old. It was at No. 21 of the CDC buildings in La Clery, a two-bedroom apartment later occupied by the Cenacs. That was before we moved to No. 7, a larger three-bedroom unit.

I had gotten in the habit of calling for my mother to let her know I was awake and ready to be helped down out of the crib and fed my bottle. But this time she didn't respond. I thought she hadn't heard me calling.

I continued to call out with whatever vocal capacity I had at that age, but still no response. My calls changed to cries and progressed to yelling and hysterics, yet no response. I was keenly aware that she, or someone, was in the kitchen, out of sight but definitely within earshot of my pleas.

I carried on the charade for what seemed like an hour and I had gotten even hungrier, and angrier. Eventually I conceded in the battle of wills proceeded to climb over the side of the crib and ease my way down safely to the ground. I walked over to the kitchen and peeked in to find my mother standing there with the feeding bottle in her hand.

"Oh, so you do know how to get out of the crib on your own," she remarked sarcastically.

Even at that tender age I recall being annoyed with my mother for deliberately ignoring my calls, but also for exposing my attempts to hide the fact that I was quite capable of climbing out of the crib and fetching my bottle. That was the last time I called for unneeded assistance.

"Lejitim" and "Bata"

"Ou kwe ou say lejitim ek Pita se bata?"

When I was a child, my mother would always utter these words to chastise me for being overly aggressive toward my brother. It would be many years later before I understood the meaning of what she was saying.

I recall that I didn't care to be "lejitim" because I could better relate to "bata." Bata was a big shoe store on Bridge Street in Castries. So if Peter was "bata," in my mind he was better off than being "lejitim." After all, I had nothing impressive to relate to "lejitim."

At some point, as I began to lose my innocence, I became rudely aware of a rule, a law in our society, that declared I was born, by fate, in violation of certain religious and state prohibitions. In other words, I was "bata" and would remain, for the rest of my life, a second-class citizen!

Shocking! Do you know what that does to a child's self-esteem?

I believe the dispossessions, from a legal standpoint, have softened if not completely changed, but the religious stigma has lingered. I remember my grandmother, a devout and selfless servant of the Roman Catholic Church, being totally distraught at my brother and me for having been declared unworthy of the sacrament of baptism by the missionary priests, by virtue of being "bata."

The Wesleyans were more compassionate, so we were baptized in the Methodist Church. Later, my grandmother would hold influence over the diocese and convince the local bishop to admit us into the Catholic Church and allow us to receive the rite of the First Holy Communion. But "bata" we would remain.

It was interesting that the stigma of "bata" appeared not to be a factor with our friends or neighbors. But in officialdom, it always seemed to crop up. Some official was always ready to insist that you sign your father's last name and not your mother's. Yet it was a rule that a "bata" was not entitled to have his father's last name.

In my early school days, my father would compel us to use his last name. I used to think it was out of pity for having brought us into this condition. But many years later as an adult, I learned that he too was "bata" and in defiance had taken his father's last name. So we signed his last name, but on all official papers we were identified by my mother's last name.

Since I had been given my father's first name, I had the identifying title of Jr. However, my title followed my first name (and not my mother's last name) and it inadvertently became my middle name, Junior.

I have since grown up to believe that all God's children are "lejitim." And if that is so, then the law that declares some "bata" and others "lejitim" cannot be based on truth. At least not within the definition of truth that I accept, which is:

"A truth, if it is TRUTH, will not keep man bound, but will set him free. It will not contradict any scriptures but will reveal an unchanging God. It will transcend all cultures and resolve social problems. Its value is ageless and its application universal; thus, it is neither limited to any time period in history nor restricted to any locality on earth. It must be practical, and reproducible, in all people at all times. By this we will know that a truth is TRUTH."

But to declare that all God's children are "lejitim" is to spit in the face of long-held rules deemed sacred, regarding the institution of marriage. In essence, it is a rejection of the western tradition of monogamy as the only legitimate form of marriage. How else can everyone be indisputably "lejitim"?

La Vwa de Pep
(The will of the people)

The night was impenetrably dark. So dark it was that through the window of the airborne Cessna even the stars seemed reluctant to shine.

The twin engines of the aircraft moaned in monotonous harmony. To Gemma it felt as though it were floating, or perhaps animatedly suspended in a black limbo. She felt tired and irritated. She and Colin were fatigued by the seven-hour flight across the Atlantic. To add to their misery, their flight out of London had arrived on the island of Barbados twenty minutes after the connecting flight to Mamiku had departed. It was little consolation that the airline officials had offered to compensate by chartering a Cessna to fly them and another hapless English couple to Mamiku, later that evening.

The twenty-minute flight from Barbados to Mamiku seemed like an eternity to Gemma. She reached into her night case, pulled out her vanity kit, then shut the case and pushed it out of the way beneath the seat in front of her. She assessed her face in the tiny mirror and began to repair the damages that the long trip had done to her makeup.

On her right, Colin was engaged in light conversation with the English couple, about the inconveniences to be tolerated when visiting the "colonies." He was himself an Englishman, and like the other couple, this was his first trip to Mamiku, Gemma's birthplace. It was at his insistence that Gemma and he were now visiting the island that she had left, embittered, thirteen years ago.

At first, Gemma had resisted the idea. She had no intention of ever returning to Mamiku. But after some coaxing she had changed her mind. Now she saw this trip as an opportunity to subtly mock those people with whom she had often been in contention. Indeed, the very people who had scorned her religiously, saying she would never make "something good" of herself. As she had then, Gemma still thought of them as narrow-minded and now wanted spitefully to show them she had "made it" without their help, and despite their malevolence. She had married Colin Iser, a wealthy English banker, and could virtually "buy off" the island if she chose to convince her husband. Yes, this would be her personal Armageddon. The climax would be her meeting with Bwamitan.

Bwamitan, her former beau, she remembered as a maudlin character, overly possessive and with little ambition. When he was not watching over her every move, he was somewhere in the village singing his pitiful songs to charitable tourists and idle natives. She still remembered the lyrics of one such imploring litany he had dedicated to her.

> Cornay moin Gemma, cornay moin
> Cornay moin Gemma, cornay moin
> Cornay moin Gemma, cornay moin
> Cornay moin doudou pa kitay moin
>
> Break my heart Gemma, break my heart
> Break my heart Gemma, break my heart
> Break my heart Gemma, break my heart
> Break my heart but never let us part

But Bwamitan was well loved by the people in the village. His simple but jovial nature had always won the sympathy of inquisitive neighbors when Gemma and he quarreled about his getting a job, or over some new lover with whom she had been. In contrast, the villagers had thought of Gemma as a heartless harlot. She had then, many lovers, a fact which was a constant pain to Bwamitan's heart.

It filled Gemma with new resentment to recall his excessive sentimentality. She had longed to be free of her circumstantial subordination. But then, Bwamitan was the only one who would proudly have her in his house as his woman. She had tolerated him only for the roof over her head, his. And so, thirteen years ago, on a night as dark as the present one, she had quietly slipped aboard the Franca-C and sailed to England, unknown to anyone on the island. She had vowed then, never to return.

> *"We are approaching Osiris Airport,"* the pilot informed the four of them.

Gemma looked out the window and through the dense darkness could see only the converging lines of light bordering the distant air strip below. The image resembled an apex of gold dust on black velvet. She settled back as the aircraft straightened its approach to the landing, gradually declined in altitude, and touched down with a loud groan. The pilot ran the aircraft for a short distance, turned it around, and taxied to the spotlighted apron.

> *"Please remain seated until both engines are turned off,"* the pilot spouted ritualistically.

Gemma's heart beat a little faster. Through the window, she could barely make out the somber silhouette of the small wooden building that served as a terminal. Adjoining it, the tower stood twice its height. The entire complex sat in the soft light that reflected from the apron. It offered no accommodation to the unscheduled arrival. There was something cryptic about its form, Gemma thought. The top of the tower seemed more like a head to the adjoining body of the terminal. It reminded Gemma of the picture of the sphinx she had seen at a photographic exhibition in Liverpool a year ago.

The pilot turned off the aircraft engines. For the first time Gemma saw the cold shaft of steel that was the propeller come to a vertical rest. It had spun invisibly when the engines were engaged.

The pilot jumped out of the cockpit onto the ground, ducked under the wing, and reappeared on the near side to open the passenger exit. The four passengers stepped out of the aircraft into the night. They claimed their luggage from the pilot, exchanged gratuities, and wearily walked toward the terminal in a broken line. Gemma lagged. She thought only of arriving at their hotel and retiring for the night.

As she approached the terminal, Gemma felt haunted by a feeling of incompleteness. She paused. Momentarily, realization came to her and at once turned to panic.

"My night case — it's still on the aircraft!" she exclaimed.

In her lassitude, Gemma had forgotten the night case beneath the seat in the aircraft. She broke into a run back to the aircraft, waving frantically at the pilot who was already seated in the cockpit and about to start off.

> *"Wait a moment, wait a moment,"* she shouted, *"my night case."*

Gemma was outside the pilot's peripheral vision, and not near enough to be heard through the cockpit glass. She reached the aircraft however, and circled to the front to catch the pilot's attention. Just then, the pilot turned on the engines. Gemma never saw the propeller begin its swing. It smashed into the left side of her face, knocking her flat onto the apron.

The rude impact of the blow caused Gemma to go unconscious. When she tried to regain herself she was barely sensible. She was not immediately aware of the pain, but she felt as though her head had been halved. The sight was gone from her left eye. Through the blood that poured like thick syrup over her right eye, she saw three white faces huddled triangularly over her.

> *"Get a taxi quick ... got to get her to the hospital ..."*
> someone was shouting in desperation.

Gemma felt the ground being pulled away from her as she slowly slipped back into unconsciousness.

◆　　◆　　◆

Someone was calling Gemma's name as she fought to surface from a deep euphoria. It was the voice of a woman; a native woman. The voice carried a fine echo which Gemma attributed more to her drunken senses than the texture of the woman's voice. Gemma noticed at the same time that she seemed to be deaf to all but the almost cherubic sounding voice.

> *"Gemma, Gemma you can hear me? ... is me, Wowena,*
> *your old friend ... you remember me?"*

It was a while before Gemma could coordinate what she heard. She forced her eyes open but received limited response from only her right eye. Through the mist of her sedation, she made out an object hanging from above. An umbilical extension ran from the object and disappeared somewhere on her left side. Gemma thought of intravenous feeding and was convinced she was in a hospital, probably the recovery room. Scenes from the accident came back to her.

> *"Ah know you can hear me Gemma. Yuh don't have to*
> *talk. Ah know you not feelin' good,"* Wowena echoed
> softly.

Gemma wondered how long she had been unconscious. Simultaneously she became flushed with thoughts of Colin. Why was he not the one at her bedside? She wanted to open her mouth to speak, but her jaws felt heavy and swollen and constrained her tongue. Unable to move her head, Gemma found she had no physical control. At least her mummified senses insulated her from pain.

> *"Don' try to move, ah go come closer,"* Wowena
> whispered as though she could read Gemma's mind.

Wowena was now staring down into Gemma's face, but Gemma's only active eye could not focus. What she perceived was a cloudy dark oval with changing contortions as Wowena spoke.

> *"Yuh remember me, Gemma? I was the only friend yuh had. I used to stan' up for yuh when everybody else drag yuh name in de gutter ..."*

Gemma remembered. Indeed, Wowena was the only one on the island whom she might have considered a friend. Wowena was always abreast of the local gossip. Through her talent for securing and disseminating information, Gemma was kept informed on all deprecations directed at her by envious neighbors who had confided in Wowena. Wowena's best gift however, was her greatest fault. She had the face of a confidante but in fact belonged to the guild of the mythical Pandora. The villagers had named her "Langue Kaka," which meant "septic tongue." Some had even joked that before "telephona" came to the island, people would simply "tel-Wowena."

Once, Gemma had revealed to Wowena her secret urge to "ship away some day." Then fearing that Wowena would carelessly relay that information, she jokingly revoked her statement.

> *"Don' listen to me gyal, ah very happy here with me man ... now what would a poor island gyal like me do in a big place like Englan'?"*

Gemma felt she had some control of her facial muscles and tugged willfully at the right side of her mouth to acknowledge Wowena's presence.

Wowena sobbed loudly. Talking through her tears, each sentence was punctuated with short outbursts.

> *"Gemma, ah so sorry dis happen to yuh ... yuh not as bad as dey say ... ah know yuh as me own sister ... but you shoulda never come back."*

Wowena's oval moved out of Gemma's view and the sobbing ceased. Gemma felt touched by Wowena's empathy. She told herself that if she recovered from her present misfortune, she would make a gift of one of her most cherished possessions to Wowena.

When Wowena started again, there was a fostering quality in her voice.

> *"Gemma, ah mean good for yuh. Yuh must leave dis islan' as soon as yuh well enough to move. It ain' nothing but evil here for yuh. Take yuh husband and go back to Englan' and don' never come back."*

Gemma felt slightly irritated by Wowena's superstition. In England, she had learned appropriate answers for such nonsense but presently she lacked the faculties to scold this "backward thinking" out of Wowena's head. It was all this superstition, she thought, that had kept these people illiterate and regressive. Gemma wanted badly to tell Wowena how ridiculous she was and how she only hurt herself by believing in this necromancy. For now, the most she could do was attempt a frown.

Wowena seemingly read the meaning of Gemma's frown and insisted.

> *"No, Gemma, yuh must listen to me. It is not nonsense. In Englan' maybe dey don't believe dat evil can hurt yuh so it don't work over there. But here, it work because de people believe in it. Remember, as children, they teach us dat 'de will of the people is de will of God' ..."*

Gemma felt her forgotten past was coming back to haunt her. She had a feeling of frustration she had known before, under Bwamitan's suffocating ordinance. She longed to see Colin and tried to call out to him, but her tongue was something foreign she could not command. She closed her eye and struggled to go back to sleep in the hope that Wowena would quit and go away. Even with her eyes closed Wowena's oval face seemed to peer through the privacy of Gemma's eyelids. Wowena sounded apocalyptic.

> *"You been blighted, Gemma. Bwamitan done blight you. When you left him he thought yuh was hiding with another man. He went to see de Obeah man and de Obeah man tell him yuh gone far far away. He asked de Obeah man to fix it so you drop dead de day yuh ever come back to dis islan'. Yuh must believe dis Gemma, and leave here like ah tell yuh."*

Wowena paused hopefully. Gemma offered no acknowledgment. Still, Wowena continued with increased urgency.

*"He ain't never been de same since. He don't talk to
nobody and he don't sing and play his guitar like he used
to. De people say yuh take his music and his laughter when
yuh left him. Dey all wish for his sake, that yuh come back
and drop dead so he can be himself again."*

Wowena seemed to be on the verge of another tearful outburst. This
was no help to the confusion that was building in Gemma's head.

*"Tell me you will go back to Englan'. Just wink yuh eye ...
yuh have to tell me now. Ah don't have much time left. Ah
done stayed too long already ..."*

Gemma felt tormented. She wanted to withdraw the little of her
senses that she was conscious of. She felt herself at the climax of a
nightmare with no escape; only, she longed to go back to sleep
rather than wake up. In her mind, she cursed Wowena and Bwamitan, and all her other ill-wishers whom she could not see. She had a
keen sense of melancholy that denied her the relief of tears. Where
was Colin? Why was he not here to comfort her in this limbo?

Gemma felt a deep slow pounding which she took to be that of her
heart. She counted twelve beats, after which she passed into a sleep
deeper than the first.

◆   ◆   ◆

Outside the emergency room in the hospital, Colin Iser, weary and disheveled, nervously rubbed the dry scales of Gemma's blood from his hands. In vain, the English couple tried to get him to relax. He took a quick glance at his watch. It was midnight, forty minutes since the accident. No one had come out of the operating theatre to report on Gemma's condition.

Almost instantly the doors to the theatre swung open. The chief surgeon emerged, looked in Colin's direction, and spoke with professional brevity.

> *"She died on the stroke of midnight. She never regained consciousness."*